My Brain

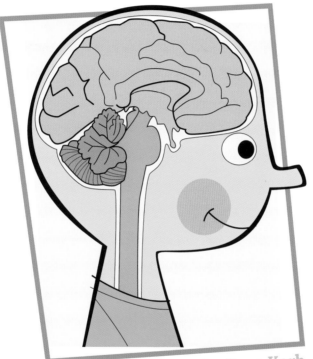

by Rena Korb

illustrated by Rémy Simard

Content Consultant:
Anthony J. Weinhaus, PhD
Assistant Professor of Integrative Biology and Physiology
University of Minnesota

visit us at www.abdopublishing.com

Printed in the United States of America, North Mankato, Minnesota.
022010
092010

 THIS BOOK CONTAINS AT LEAST 10% RECYCLED MATERIALS.

Text by Rena Korb
Illustrations by Rémy Simard
Edited by Holly Saari
Interior layout and design by Emily Love
Cover design by Emily Love

Library of Congress Cataloging-in-Publication Data
Korb, Rena B.
 My brain / by Rena Korb ; illustrated by Remy Simard ; content consultant, Anthony J. Weinhaus.
    p. cm. — (My body)
 Includes index.
 ISBN 978-1-60270-805-1
 1. Brain—Juvenile literature. 2. Neurophysiology—Juvenile literature. I. Simard, Rémy, ill. II. Weinhaus, Anthony J. III. Title.
 QP376.K653 2011
 612.8'2—dc22

                    2009048309

Table of Contents

My Brain

Hi! I'm Jake. I have a twin brother. You might think that makes us exactly alike. But we're not.

When I see a dog, I pet it. When my brother sees a dog, he runs away. Our brains make us different. Let's learn more about brains!

My brain is in charge of everything I do. It lets me breathe, move, and feel. It lets me think and talk. My brain is why I can tell you about my brain!

An adult's brain is about the size of a large grapefruit. But it looks more like a grayish-pink walnut.

My brain is soft and squishy.
Luckily, it's inside my hard skull.
That keeps it safe in case I bump
my head.

The cranium is the part of the
skull that keeps the brain safe.
It has eight bones. The whole
skull has 22 bones.

My brain sends messages to
my whole body. How does my hand
know to wave good-bye? My brain
tells it to wave.

A special part of your brain makes you grow.
This part is called the pituitary gland. It is
only about the size of a pea.

My brain also gets messages. Nerves all over my body tell my brain what's going on around me.

I've lost my mouse. Where is it? I feel inside my desk drawer. I grab something. Nerves in my fingers send my brain a message. Then, my brain figures out what I'm holding. I found my mouse!

Nerves work very fast. It takes just a split second for messages to travel to your brain.

My brain lets me decide what to do. My brother and I play soccer. He kicks the ball to me. What is my next move? I decide to stop the ball. Then my brain tells my foot how.

The brain controls whether you are right-handed or left-handed. Some people can use either of their hands to write or throw a baseball.

My brain has three main parts. The brain stem keeps me alive. It makes my heart beat, my lungs breathe, and my eyes blink. I don't control my brain stem.

The brain stem sends messages to the body even when a person is sleeping.

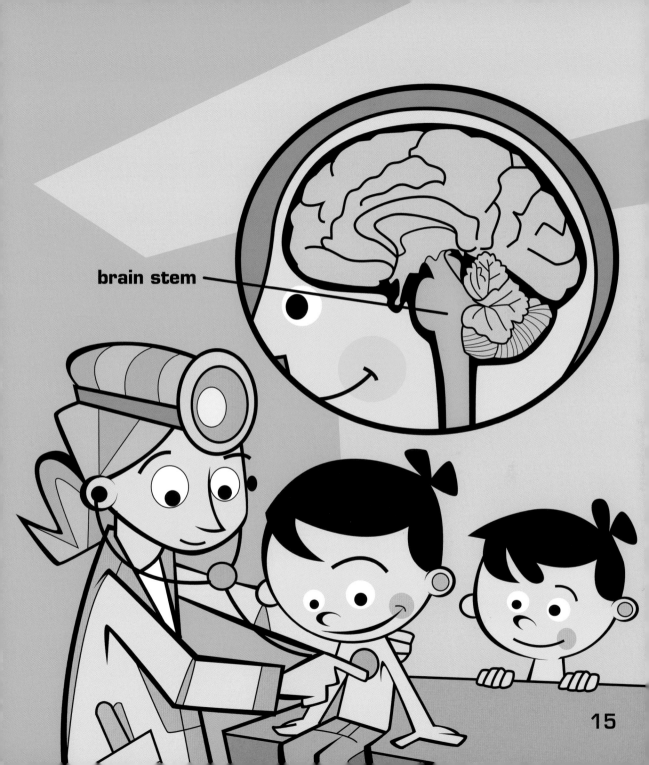

brain stem

The cerebellum is the part of my brain that helps me move. It also helps me keep my balance. This part works on its own, like the brain stem.

The cerebellum keeps you under control. It's the reason you don't tear a page out of a book as you turn it. It lets you scratch your nose without cutting yourself.

cerebellum

17

The cerebrum is the largest part of my brain. It does not work totally on its own. My cerebrum lets me think, learn, and control some muscles.

A baby's brain is much smaller than an adult's brain. But by the time the baby is two, his or her brain is almost fully grown.

cerebrum

19

My cerebrum stores my memories. It also lets me feel. I remember a new classmate's name. I'm happy to see her!

The brain decides what is important to remember. Then it files the information to use later.

Because of my cerebrum, I can solve problems. I build a sand castle. But the water ruins it. My cerebrum figures out that I should build a moat!

People can train their brains. Learning new words or solving riddles helps the brain work better.

I learn new things all the time because of my brain. When I try something new, I have to think hard.

A good night's sleep can help you better remember what you learned during the day.

My brain builds on what I already know. When I do a puzzle, I already know that the straight pieces go on the outside.

It's easier to learn new things when you are younger. Older people can keep their brains in good shape by doing crossword puzzles or playing memory games.

My brain has a big job to do. It keeps my body working every day. My brain also makes me special. There is no one in the world who is exactly like me!

Keep your brain healthy by eating well and learning new things. Protect your brain by wearing a helmet when you ride a bike or a skateboard.

A Look Inside

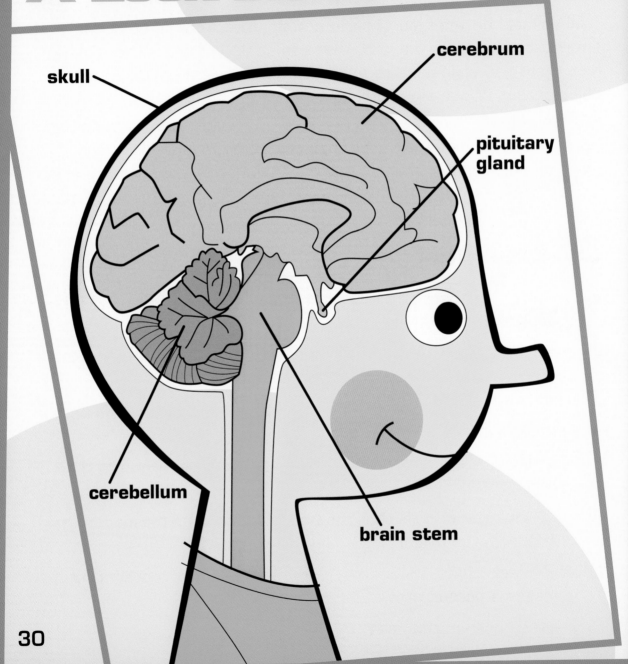

skull

cerebrum

pituitary gland

cerebellum

brain stem

Fun Facts

• All animals have a type of brain. Chimpanzees are some of the smartest animals. In the wild, they use sticks as tools. The tools help them gather insects to eat. Scientists have even taught some chimpanzees to use sign language.

• The cerebrum is divided into two halves. The left half controls the right side of the body. The right half controls the left side of the body. In most people, the left side controls things like speaking and understanding words. The right side lets people create art and music.

Glossary

brain stem – the part of the brain that controls breathing and other actions that keep a person alive.

cerebellum (sehr-uh-BEH-luhm) – the part of the brain that helps with balance and movement.

cerebrum (suh-REE-bruhm) – the part of the brain that lets a person think, learn, remember, and feel.

cranium (KRAY-nee-uhm) – the part of the skull that protects the brain.

nerves – clusters of cells that the body uses to send messages to and from the brain.

pituitary [puh-TOO-uh-tehr-ee] gland – the part of the brain that makes a person grow.

skull – the bones in the head.

31

On the Web

To learn more about the brain, visit **ABDO Group** online at www.abdopublishing.com. Web sites about the brain are featured on our Book Links page. These links are routinely monitored and updated to provide the most current information available.

Index